WOMEN RULERS

HIDDEN IN HISTORY

Sarah Eason

CRABTREE
Publishing Company
www.crabtreebooks.com

T0019658

Author: Sarah Eason

Editorial director: Kathy Middleton

Editors: Jennifer Sanderson, Ellen Rodger

Proofreaders: Jennifer Sanderson, Jillian Harvey

Design: Paul Myerscough and Jessica Moon

Cover design: Emma DeBanks and Jessica Moon

Illustrations: Jessica Moon

Photo research: Rachel Blount

Production coordinator and
  Prepress technician: Margaret Amy Salter

Print coordinator: Katherine Berti

Written, developed, and produced by Calcium

Photo Credits:

t=Top, c=Center, b=Bottom, l= Left, r=Right

Inside: Shutterstock: Aphotostory: p. 27;
Kotinov Baatr: p. 26b; Beibaoke: pp. 20, 25;
Iconic Bestiar: p. 18t; Bist: p. 34; Myroslava
Bozhko: p. 5; Josep Curto: p. 11; D-Visions:
p. 36b; DC Aperture: p. 29; DiPetre: pp. 36-
37; Emperorcosar: p. 9; Everett Historical:
p. 18b; Gilmanshin: p. 39; HappyPictures:
p. 7b; Insideportugal: p. 10; Iakov Kalinin:
p. 15; Kamnuan: p. 42; Marzolino: p. 13;
Microgen: p. 7t; Shane Myers Photography:
p. 33; Sophy Ru: p. 23; Brigida Soriano:
p. 45; Takito: p. 16l; Torwai Studio: p. 30,
Vkilikov: p. 17; Wikimedia Commons:
Louis le Grand: p 41t; PHGCOM: p. 41b.

Library and Archives Canada Cataloguing in Publication

Title: Women rulers : hidden in history / Sarah Eason.
Names: Eason, Sarah, author.
Description: Series statement: Hidden history | Includes index.
Identifiers: Canadiana (print) 20200153242 |
  Canadiana (ebook) 20200153250 |
  ISBN 9780778772996 (hardcover) |
  ISBN 9780778773061 (softcover) |
  ISBN 9781427124777 (HTML)
Subjects: LCSH: Women heads of state—Biography—
  Juvenile literature. | LCSH: Women heads of state—
  History—Juvenile literature.
Classification: LCC D107.3 E27 2020 | DDC j920.72—dc23

Library of Congress Cataloging-in-Publication Data

Names: Eason, Sarah, author.
Title: Women rulers hidden in history / Sarah Eason.
Description: New York : Crabtree Publishing Company, [2020] |
  Series: Hidden history | Includes bibliographical references and
  index.
Identifiers: LCCN 2019054367 (print) | LCCN 2019054368 (ebook)
  ISBN 9780778772996 (hardcover) |
  ISBN 9780778773061 (paperback) | ISBN 9781427124777 (ebook)
Subjects: LCSH: Queens--History--Juvenile literature. |
  Women heads of state--History--Juvenile literature.
Classification: LCC D107.3 E375 2020 (print) |
  LCC D107.3 (ebook) | DDC 352.23092/2 [B]--dc23
LC record available at https://lccn.loc.gov/2019054367
LC ebook record available at https://lccn.loc.gov/2019054368

Crabtree Publishing Company
www.crabtreebooks.com   1-800-387-7650

Printed in the U.S.A./022020/CG20200102

Published in Canada
Crabtree Publishing
616 Welland Ave.
St. Catharines, Ontario
L2M 5V6

Published in the United States
Crabtree Publishing
PMB 59051
350 Fifth Avenue, 59th Floor
New York, New York 10118

Published in the United Kingdom
Crabtree Publishing
Maritime House
Basin Road North, Hove
BN41 1WR

Published in Australia
Crabtree Publishing
Unit 3 - 5 Currumbin Court
Capalaba
QLD 4157

CONTENTS

HISTORY'S HIDDEN HEROINES

There are many stories from ancient history about the great rulers of our past. In ancient cultures, people often believed the world had to be ruled by men and that women should have little power. More recently, that view has begun to change.

Powerful Today

In the twenty-first century, we have many examples of female rulers, such as Germany's **chancellor** Angela Merkel. Elsewhere in Europe, women are leading the way too—Denmark has elected women prime ministers, as has Poland. South America, Argentina, Chile, and Brazil have all had female presidents. In Africa, the Central African Republic had a female president, Catherine Samba-Panza. But were there great female leaders in the ancient world too?

Digging Up the Past

When we study history, we learn about some well-**recorded** women rulers, such as England's Elizabeth I and Queen Victoria. We can see that they ruled their countries with skill and strength. But there were also other women rulers who are less well known and many of them were formidable leaders. They took on enemies, built up their countries, and showed the men around them that they were no pushovers!

Queen Victoria is an example of a great and famous woman ruler, but were there others like her who are less well known?

4

We are now learning more and more about great female rulers of the past, women who wowed the ancient world with their **authority** and smart thinking. But how is it that these awesome women are so little known? Why have their stories not been as widely told as those of male leaders? To answer these questions, we need to look at how history has been recorded.

OLYMPIAS, THE POWER MOM!

Sometimes, women ruled from behind the men! For example, we know of the powerful ancient Greek ruler Alexander the Great, but did you know that his rise to power was in part due to his mighty mom? Olympias was mother to Alexander, and many say she was the brain behind her son, helping him rise to power, and stay there.

This is a statue of Olympias (left) and her son Alexander (right). Even after Alexander's death, Olympias was determined to keep her grandson, Alexander's son, on the throne, so she killed anyone who threatened him.

So, Why Can't We Read All About It?

In very ancient history, before **civilizations** started to take over other peoples, women often had important positions in their communities. They had power as religious leaders, they helped make important decisions about the futures of their people, and they took leadership roles. Women often offered peaceful solutions to problems and helped knit together their communities.

Everything Changes

Some historians believe that women's power began to change with the spread of agriculture, or farming, which began around 9000 BCE. For reasons that are not fully understood, this change meant that the power to make decisions shifted to men. Some think that wars over good farming land broke out, and men became powerful as fighters. Others think that the heavy, physical work of farming made men's work more valuable. Another idea is that at this time, people began to live in one place, rather than moving around. When people had traveled around, women had often chosen where the group would set up a new camp. This stopped when people started farming in one place, and meant that women lost some of their power. As agriculture spread, men became more likely to be rulers and women less so.

There are lots of legends and stories about great male rulers, like that of King Arthur of Britain, but far fewer about women. Why might that be?

Women—Why Write About Them?

As civilizations grew and changed, men took more and more power. They made decisions for their **societies**, and women were not allowed to be as involved in decision making as they may have been in the past. Leadership was held by men, who became kings and emperors. That leadership was then passed down to the sons of kings and emperors. Very rarely would a daughter be allowed power, and usually only if there was no son to rule or if the daughter was determined enough to seize control.

Men also became powerful because they had the job of recording, or writing down, history. And because men no longer believed that women should have power, they often did not write about powerful women. That is an important reason why great women rulers are often little known today.

Historians and **archaeologists** are now on the hunt to find more great women rulers whose stories might lie buried in the past.

Historians Hunting Heroines

To set the record straight, historians are now trying to find out more about women rulers of the past. They are discovering great women leaders and finding out how they changed their worlds. They are also learning that in some cultures, women had a lot of power and often ruled their people.

As we hunt for history, amazing women rulers are rising up from the past, and they have awesome stories to tell. Let's read about some of them!

In the past, history was often recorded by men, such as monks, and they wrote mainly about other men rather than women.

CHAPTER 2

EPIC IN EUROPE

We may know a lot about the great kings of Europe, but this continent also had some epic queens. Some were incredible leaders, others were hidden heroines, but they all have secrets to tell ...

Isabella, the Cool-headed Queen

When she was born in 1451, it looked unlikely that Isabella of Castile, a kingdom in Spain, would become a queen, let alone the greatest queen in Europe. Yet through her cool thinking and icy determination, Isabella went on to rule her country and go down in history as one of the greatest leaders of her age.

You Will Never Be Queen

Isabella was the daughter of King John II of Castile. No one thought Isabella would ever rule because John already had an **heir**, his son Henry, who was Isabella's half-bother. John also had a second son, Alfonso, so Isabella was third in line to the throne. When John died in 1454, Henry became king.

Isabella did not look like a fighter: people who saw her commented that she was slim and slight. However, the feisty princess had a will of iron and never gave up in a fight.

When Henry became king, he made Isabella live with him in the palace at Segovia, where he could keep her under his control.

Who Will Rule?

When Henry had a daughter, named Joanna, he said that she would be queen when he died. Some powerful people in Henry's court did not believe that Henry was a good ruler. They also believed that Henry could not have children, so they thought that Joanna was not his child but the daughter of another man. When Joanna was named next in line to rule, these powerful men backed Henry's brother Alfonso and said he should be king instead.

Isabella saw the growing quarrel as her chance to shake things up, so she backed Alfonso too. Fighting between Henry and Alfonso broke out, and Alfonso declared himself king. Alfonso never officially became king, but before he died in 1468 he named Isabella his heir.

HIDDEN HISTORY

Secretly Hating Henry

Some historians think that Isabella secretly hated Henry because he forced her to leave her mother and move away to live with him in the city of Segovia, from where he ruled. It is possible that Isabella never forgave him for that.

Biding Her Time

Rather than make a move immediately, Isabella bided her time after Alfonso's death. She knew that Henry would likely try to marry her off to a husband he thought would control her, so she chose to make her own match. The partner she chose was Ferdinand II, the king of the powerful Spanish state of Aragon. Isabella sneakily married Ferdinand in secret.

By making her own marriage, Isabella showed the signs of the strength that would go on to make her the greatest queen of her age. This statue of the queen and her husband, Ferdinand, stands in Malaga, Spain.

HIDDEN HISTORY

A Secret Prenup

When Isabella was arranging her marriage to Ferdinand, she insisted that he sign a secret **prenuptial** agreement. It said that he would allow Isabella to be the chief ruler of Castile and would not interfere in her decision making. Isabella was determined to marry a husband who would not try to control her.

The Power Couple

Isabella's marriage made her extremely powerful. By combining the power of Castile with Aragon, Isabella had created a great **alliance**, and one that could easily stand up to her brother Henry. But in the end, Isabella had no need to fight with Henry, because he died in 1474. Isabella quickly named herself the ruler of Castile and then went to war against Joanna, Henry's daughter.

Aragon was a wealthy Spanish kingdom with great cities and towns such as Alquézar, shown here.

A Modern Marriage

For the next four years of their marriage, Isabella and Ferdinand fought a war against Joanna. Isabella soon showed that she wouldn't be pushed around in war, or in marriage. She took one half of the army under her control, and Ferdinand took the other half. It was a marriage of equals.

Isabella spent years fighting the war and many days riding around her lands to gain control of them. Her efforts paid off, and by 1479 Isabella and Ferdinand had defeated Joanna. A year later, Ferdinand's father died, and Ferdinand and Isabella were crowned king and queen of Aragon. Castile and Aragon now had the same rulers, and this was the beginning of a united, or joined-as-one, country, Spain.

Dark Determination

There was a dark side to Isabella's determination to control Spain. In 1480 she and Ferdinand set up the Spanish Inquisition. This was an organization led by **Catholic priests** who were determined to make everyone in Spain Catholic. The inquisition questioned anyone it thought might not be a good Catholic, including Jews, **Muslims**, and **Protestants**. People might be **tortured** to make them say they went against Catholic beliefs. They might then be put in prison or killed.

One Land, One People

Isabella went on to unify Spain by forcing the Muslim **conquerors** to leave the country. The Muslims of North Africa had invaded Spain many years before the rule of Isabella and they controlled lands in the south. Isabella was determined to make Spain one land again, with only Christians as its people. She set about forcing the Muslim rulers in southern Spain from power and by 1492 had taken back their lands.

THE WARRIOR QUEEN

Isabella saw herself as a powerful warrior queen—she even kept a book about the famous **medieval** French warrior Joan of Arc on her bookshelf. She oversaw the training and organization of her army and came up with battle plans for it. She also made sure her army had the best of weapons so that it was virtually unstoppable.

Isabella was a fan of other great women! She particularly admired the famous warrior Joan of Arc (shown here).

Isabella's investment in Columbus (see below) changed modern history. By backing Columbus, she helped bring about the discovery of new lands. This illustration shows Columbus arriving in America.

Changing the World

In 1492, Isabella met an ambitious explorer who would change Spain's future and the future of the entire Western world. His name was Christopher Columbus. Isabella was excited by Columbus's plans to discover new, wealthy lands, and she gave him money to pay for his trips. This was the first of a number of trips that eventually led to Columbus sailing to America. The lands in America later claimed by Spain made both the country and Isabella even more powerful.

A Spanish Superpower

By the time Isabella died in 1504, she had turned Spain into a united country. She had made it a superpower with a mighty army, a powerful fleet of ships, and many rich new lands overseas. Not bad for a girl who no one thought would ever be queen.

Elizabeth I, Single-minded and Single

Elizabeth I was one of England's greatest queens and her **reign** has become famous in history. Even today, the time in which she ruled is seen as so important that it is known as the "Elizabethan Age."

Famous Family

Elizabeth first came to the throne in 1558, when she was just 25 years old. Up until this point, Elizabeth was famous only as the redheaded daughter of her larger-than-life father, King Henry VIII. She was also the half-sister of Mary I, who was queen before her.

So Much for Sisterhood

Mary was very jealous of Elizabeth, because she thought she was prettier and more popular than herself. She also believed Elizabeth wanted to be queen. So Mary locked Elizabeth in a prison called the Tower of London.

Luckily for Elizabeth, Mary died in 1558, before she could harm her half-sister. Elizabeth then became queen.

Her imprisonment must have been a terrifying time for Elizabeth—many prisoners in the Tower were killed.

A Difficult Start

The drama was far from over for Elizabeth when she came to the throne because England was in a bit of a mess. Both Henry VIII and Mary I had spent a lot of money during their reigns and there was very little left in the royal bank.

The people of England were also unhappy—they had seen Elizabeth's father crush the Catholic Church in England and create a new one, the Church of England. When Mary took over, she tried to make England Catholic again and burned many Protestants.

Savvy and Smart

There were also problems overseas, with many countries threatening England, including the superpower Spain. Elizabeth had to quickly deal with all of these problems. Luckily for her, she was tough, super-smart, and able to run rings around her enemies.

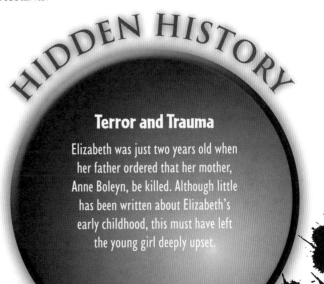

HIDDEN HISTORY

Terror and Trauma

Elizabeth was just two years old when her father ordered that her mother, Anne Boleyn, be killed. Although little has been written about Elizabeth's early childhood, this must have left the young girl deeply upset.

15

You Choose!

Elizabeth knew that to keep people happy she needed to allow them to be either Protestant or Catholic—whichever they chose. She had just one rule: people who wanted to be Catholic had to practice their **faith** in private.

Undercover Queen

Elizabeth rarely trusted anyone and chose her helpers (called advisors) very carefully. She handpicked men that she knew were very smart and whom she could trust. Her closest advisor was Sir Francis Walsingham, who was also known as the "spymaster." Walsingham used many spies to find out what was going on in England and abroad—in fact, Elizabeth had the biggest **spy network** in Europe!

Elizabeth allowed Catholics to pray with priests, but only if they did so in secret.

Even the powerful king of Spain, Philip II, wanted to marry Elizabeth. But rather than marry, Elizabeth told her people that she was already happily married—to them and England! Why do you think this was a smart use of words?

Who Needs a Husband?

Elizabeth knew that her people wanted her to marry. If she married, it meant she could have a baby who could one day become king. Elizabeth's advisors regularly introduced princes and kings who offered to marry her. But Elizabeth was determined to be single. She knew that if she married, her husband would want to rule her country—and herself. And this cunning queen wasn't having that!

Keep Them Dangling!

Elizabeth also knew that the promise of marriage was a powerful card she could play. She flirted with many powerful princes and kings, including the great king of Spain, Philip II. Elizabeth made them all think that she might marry them. Playing hard to get helped Elizabeth keep many countries friendly with England, because their rulers thought she might one day become their wife.

A WAY WITH WORDS

Elizabeth was a great speaker and used words as weapons. She often told her advisors that she was just a simple woman who needed their help. This made them think she was doing what they wanted, when all along Elizabeth actually had her own ideas.

Image Is Everything

Elizabeth knew that how people saw her was very important, so she kept total control of her image. If Instagram had been around when Elizabeth was alive, she would have had millions of followers! She had artists make many paintings of her that all showed her as a magnificent ruler, covered in jewels and looking all-powerful.

The Other Queen

Elizabeth was also threatened by another queen—her cousin, Mary, Queen of Scots. Mary was a threat because some people believed she had a greater **claim** to the English throne than Elizabeth. Mary was the granddaughter of Henry VIII's sister, Mary. Enemies of Elizabeth said that her mother, Anne Boleyn, had never been properly married to Henry VIII. They claimed that Elizabeth was **illegitimate**, and Mary was the true queen.

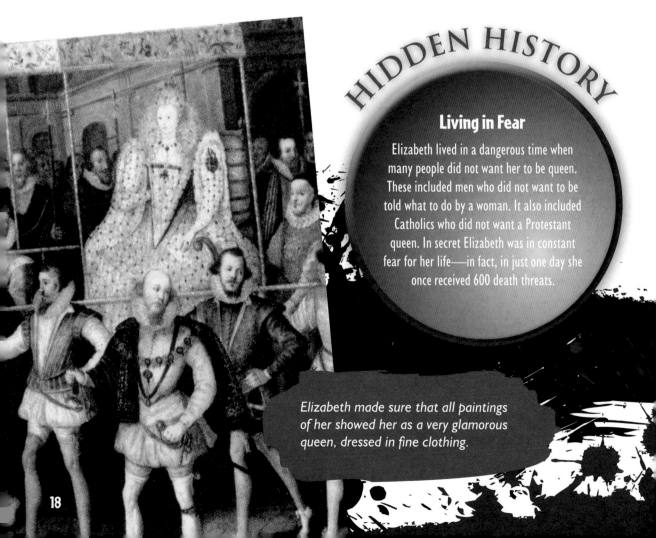

HIDDEN HISTORY

Living in Fear

Elizabeth lived in a dangerous time when many people did not want her to be queen. These included men who did not want to be told what to do by a woman. It also included Catholics who did not want a Protestant queen. In secret Elizabeth was in constant fear for her life—in fact, in just one day she once received 600 death threats.

Elizabeth made sure that all paintings of her showed her as a very glamorous queen, dressed in fine clothing.

Two Queens, One Survivor

Elizabeth was very scared that Mary might try to invade England and claim the crown for herself. To protect herself, Elizabeth had Mary captured and locked up in Fotheringay Castle in England. She held Mary there for around 19 years.

When a **plot** showing that Mary might be trying to get rid of Elizabeth was discovered, she felt she had no choice but to sign Mary's **death warrant**. In the end, Elizabeth knew that only one queen could survive—and she made sure that it was herself.

Famous Forever

Elizabeth used her smart thinking to build an England that was far stronger by the end of her reign than it was when she came to power. Elizabeth reigned for 45 glorious years, and by the time she died in 1603 she had become England's most famous queen.

*Mary, Queen of Scots was **beheaded** in 1587.*

There are many amazing women who ruled in Asia. Here are just some of these incredible greats of the East.

Wu Zetian, Super-scary Empress

Wu Zetian was an extraordinary empress of China, who was born in 624 CE and died around 705 CE. Wu is famous for being a ruthless woman who would do anything to get and keep power, including killing her own children! But how much of this is really true? And is that all she should be remembered for?

Climbing up the Ladder

Wu's climb to power began when she was just a teenager. She came from a rich and **noble** family and had been well educated as a girl. By the time she was 13 years old, she had become the favorite girlfriend of the emperor, Daizong. But Wu also had eyes for his son, Gaozong.

The emperor died when Wu was 27 years old. Wu then became Gaozong's consort, which is a female companion, and had several sons with him. But Wu wanted to be more than a consort.

This statue shows Wu and Gaozong.

I Will Be Empress!

When Wu and Gaozong had a baby girl, she tragically died soon after birth. It was then that Wu came up with a plot to get rid of Gaozong's wife, the Empress Wang. Wu told Gaozong that Wang had killed their newborn baby daughter. Gaozong believed her and left Wang. He then made Wu empress of China.

HIDDEN HISTORY

An Evil Baby Killer!

Enemies of Wu did not believe that Wang had killed her daughter. Instead, they believed that Wu had killed her own baby to get power. However, there is no proof to show that this is true. It is more likely that Wu simply used the tragic death of her baby to turn Gaozong against Wang.

Why do you think historians from ancient China and other people of the time might have liked to believe that Wu was a wicked baby killer? What does this tell us about people's attitudes toward ambitious women?

Wu Moves In

A few years after Wu became empress, Gaozong had a stroke and was unable to rule. Wu saw her chance to become even more powerful. She took control of the court and even put a spy network in place to make sure she knew everybody's business. If anyone got in Wu's way or complained about her, she found out about it. And those people often found themselves in prison or worse, dead!

Do What Your Mommy Says!

Wu knew that people in ancient China would want her sons to rule rather than herself, so she made her youngest and easiest-to-control son ruler, but she still told him what to do! In 690 CE, Wu's youngest son had had enough and gave up power completely, and Wu took over as the official emperor of China. It was then that she began to show herself as a super-smart politician and a great ruler.

HIDDEN HISTORY

Girl Power

One less-known fact about Wu was that she pushed for women's **rights**, allowing women to use their pre-marriage names for the first time in Chinese history. She also gave women **legal** powers. Wu believed that women could be great rulers, and in fact claimed that the perfect ruler guided her people like a mother watched over her children.

Wu was a very powerful woman. She was feared by people in the court and seen as a ruthless ruler who had total control of her people.

Wu saw the written word as more powerful than the sword. She valued education in people and saw it as the future for her country.

Show Me Your Résumé!

Wu changed the way the Chinese government worked by making sure that only well-educated people could get powerful jobs. Before Wu's time, just people from the **aristocracy** were allowed to **govern**. Many of them were high up in the army and were better at fighting than they were at running the country.

To change things up, Wu made sure that anyone who wanted to be in government passed exams to prove that he or she was smart enough for the job. She wanted the best people in control, so that only good decisions would be made.

Less Brawn, More Buildings

Wu also cut back the size of China's army, so she could spend money on other things that she saw as more important. This included building magnificent cities that impressed any foreign travelers who came to China.

Helping the Poor

Wu also worked on making the lives of ordinary people better. She cut back on the amount of **taxes** that poor people had to pay and brought in new machines that helped farmers work more **productively**. She also spent money on setting up schools so that many more Chinese people could be educated.

You Take Over Now!

As Wu went into old age, she started to give up some of her iron grip on China. She didn't use her secret spy network as much as she had in the past and by the time she became 80, she finally gave up power and allowed her third son to rule. That same year, Wu died.

No Worse than Any Man

Wu's achievements as a ruler have been overshadowed by the bad press she has had at the hands of male historians, who have written mainly about her ruthlessness. But when we look at what Wu did, we need to look at the whole picture. If Wu was ruthless, was she any more so than other male rulers of her time? Probably not.

Wu has been called wicked by historians, when many male rulers who were just like Wu are remembered as powerful and strong.

HIDDEN HISTORY

Changing the Story

It is important to remember that, like in many other parts of the ancient world, the men in ancient China did not like the idea of a woman in charge. It is likely that Wu's rule was shaped by male historians who wrote bad things about her at the time, and after her death, because they did not like the idea of a great female ruler.

A Tomb Not Fit for an Emperor

When Wu's tomb was confirmed in 1960, historians were surprised to see that there was no **epitaph**, despite the fact that Wu had been a great ruler. This may be further proof that she was disliked because she was a powerful female. Were the men that buried Wu trying to erase, or remove, her from history by not giving her an epitaph?

Wu, One of History's Hidden Heroines

We now know from studying history in detail that Wu achieved many great things in her time and **modernized** China. She left the country a far better place at her death than it was when she came to power. Perhaps all her many great achievements should be what she is best remembered for.

This statue of Wu at Huangze Temple in Sichuan, China, shows her as a powerful leader.

Mandukhai Khatun, as Great as Ghenghis

Who hasn't heard of Ghenghis Khan, the legendary powerful **Mongol** leader who conquered many lands? But have you heard of Mandukhai Khatun? Probably not, and yet this awe-inspiring woman was such a great Mongol leader that she has been called the "second Genghis Khan."

Taking on a Tattered Empire

Mandukhai lived from 1445 to 1510 and was wife to the Mongol emperor Dayan Khan. Mandukhai was older than Dayan, and after they were married, she took up the reins and began to rule.

At the time of Mandukhai and Dayan, the once-great Mongol empire had fallen into a mess. Most of the land the Mongols had previously taken from the Chinese had been taken back. And instead of being great warriors, the Mongols were fighting among themselves for scraps of land, or rebelling against their rulers. Mandukhai set out to change all that.

Mandukhai (above) was also known as Mandukhai Sechen Khatun. "Khatun" is the female form of the word Khan, and she was so-named because the Mongols believed her to be as great as the awesome Genghis Khan (left).

Mandukhai the Super Mom!

Mandukhai gathered an army of warriors and rode out onto the **steppes** to take on the troublesome Oirat tribe, which had risen against her. Mandukhai determinedly defeated the tribe and brought it back under her control. She even fought while she was pregnant with twins—only breaking from battling to give birth.

A Great Ruler Equals a Great Wall

The Oirat were not the only problem that Mandukhai had to deal with. The Ming Dynasty, the then rulers of China, also led attacks against her. Mandukhai bravely fought them off, and quickly got a reputation as an impressive warrior queen.

Who's the Wisest of Them All?

Historians think that Mandukhai died in around 1510, when she was about 60 years old. By the time of her death, she had reunited the Mongol tribes and held the throne firmly so that her husband could rule. She had become famous and loved among her people, who named her the Wise Queen.

HIDDEN HISTORY

A Secret Grave

No one knows where Mandukhai is buried. The Mongols always keep the grave of their great leaders a secret, so her burial place has never been found. It is likely that she is buried somewhere in the huge steppe lands of Mongolia.

The ancient Chinese were so worried about Mandukhai that they set about rebuilding the Great Wall of China to keep her out of their country!

CHAPTER 4

AMAZING

IN THE AMERICAS

The Americas have had many great women leaders. Some have been famous and powerful warrior queens. Others are less well known and have trodden a more peaceful path to protect their people. But they all helped shape the worlds in which they lived.

Masterful Mayan Queens

The Maya are famous for their fearsome warriors and powerful kings, but they also had some pretty impressive women. Two of them were Lady Six Sky and Lady Snake Lord.

Lady Six Sky lived from 667 to 741 CE. She was born into a Mayan royal family, in the city of Dos Pilas. When she was very young, her parents sent her to the Mayan capital, Naranjo, which had become weak and chaotic. Lady Six Sky's parents hoped that as she grew older she would be able to make the city great again.

The Birth of Girl Power

Although Lady Six Sky had an older brother, her parents still chose her to rule Naranjo. This was very unusual for the time, because power was almost always passed down to sons rather than daughters.

As Lady Six Sky grew older, she became a powerful warrior queen who easily defeated any enemies who attacked her city. She built Naranjo into a powerful capital once more. And when her son came to power, she helped him rule until she died.

Images of Lady Six Sky show her as a mighty queen, wearing fabulous clothing and sometimes holding snakes.

These are the ruins of an ancient Mayan city. Both Lady Six Sky and Lady Snake Lord would have ruled over magnificent Mayan cities like this one.

Getting the Top Job

Another great Mayan queen was Lady Snake Lord. She ruled the Wak kingdom with her husband, K'inich Bahlam II, for 20 years (672 to 692 CE). Lady Snake Lord was very special among Mayan queens—she was such a great battle planner that she was made **military commander** of her kingdom. Lady Snake Lord's job was the most important position in the kingdom. It even made her more important than her husband the king!

HIDDEN HISTORY

Lost in the Jungle

In October 2012 a team of archaeologists discovered Lady Snake Lord's tomb at the Mayan royal city of Waka. Inside the tomb the team found her body and a treasure trove of jewels. It was a truly great discovery because the tomb had been lost in the jungle for hundreds of years.

29

Nanyehi, a Beloved Leader

Nanyehi was born into a powerful **Cherokee** family in 1738, in Tennessee. As a little girl, she was terrified of European **settlers** because they attacked her people. But Nanyehi was also wary of other Indigenous nations, because they too threatened the Cherokee. These fears affected her a lot, and she longed to live peacefully. This early desire later helped shape her into a powerful peacekeeping woman.

Mother, Wife, and Warrior

When she grew up, Nanyehi married a Cherokee man named Kingfisher. For some time she lived a normal life and raised a family. But in 1755 her husband was caught up in a fight against the Creek people in Georgia. Then everything changed for Nanyehi.

Nanyehi helped in the battle, at first by keeping her husband supplied with bullets. But when he was killed in the fighting, she picked up his gun and raced to fight the enemy. Nanyehi's bravery moved the Cherokee warriors around her, so much so that they fought even harder and won the battle.

Nanyehi's actions won her the respect of her fellow Cherokee warriors.

The Beloved Woman

After the battle, Nanyehi was given the title of Beloved Woman. This was a great honor, because the Cherokee believed that a powerful spirit named the Great Spirit spoke through the Beloved Woman. Nanyehi was asked to sit on the council of chiefs and was also made head of the women's council. These were important roles because in them Nanyehi guided her people and shaped their futures.

Nanyehi helped lead the Cherokee people for many years. All that time, she worked very hard to improve relationships between her tribe and the settlers. She is remembered today as a great leader who always tried to bring about peace.

Nanyehi was also known as War Woman after her battle in Georgia, but she was most interested in fighting for peace.

KEEPING THE PEACE

All her life Nanyehi was focused on peacekeeping and caring for people. She once even saved a female settler from being burned alive by Indigenous men who were angry about the attacks by settlers.

Liluokalani, the First and Last Hawaiian Queen

Lydia Kamakaeha was born in Hawaii in 1838. She came from an important Hawaiian family and her mother worked for the then-king of Hawaii, King Kamehameha III.

Becoming Queen

In 1874 Lydia's brother, David Kalakaua, was chosen as Hawaii's next king. When Lydia's other brother died in 1877, she became next in line to the throne. From then on she became known by her royal name, Liluokalani. In January 1891 King David also died and Liluokalani then became queen.

When Liluokalani became queen, it was an important moment in history—she was the first woman to ever rule Hawaii.

Making It Count

Queen Liluokalani wanted to make her rule count, and she wanted to make Hawaii a great kingdom. During her brother's reign, Hawaii had lost a lot of power to the United States. It was forced to hand over the port of Pearl Harbor. At the same time, the U.S. government was also making moves to make the island part of the United States. Liluokalani wanted to do something about that—she was determined to keep Hawaii independent.

From Bad to Worse

Many people in Hawaii were not happy about Liluokalani's hope to keep the island free from the United States. In 1893 Hawaii's Missionary Party, led by a man named Sanford Dole, ordered that she be removed from power. Rather than have a queen and keep Hawaii independent, the party and Dole wanted the island to become part of the United States and be ruled by a government.

Asking for Help

With no one to help her, Liluokalani had no choice but to turn to the U.S. president, Glover Cleveland. He stepped in and ordered that Liluokalani be allowed to remain queen. But Dole and the Missionary Party were not eager to give in. Instead, they had Liluokalani arrested and held prisoner. Supporters of Liluokalani rallied and it soon looked like war might break out in Hawaii. To avoid bloodshed, in 1895, Liluokalani stepped down as queen and **abdicated**. It was a sad end for the first and only queen of Hawaii.

Liluokalani wanted to keep the beautiful islands of Hawaii a free kingdom.

HIDDEN HISTORY

Hidden from the Public

After her abdication, Liluokalani turned away from public life. Having lost her crown and her great hopes for Hawaii, she chose to live peacefully and away from the criticism and pressure that had been part of her reign. She lived quietly until she died in 1917.

CHAPTER 5

ACING IT IN AFRICA

Africa has been home to many powerful kings, but it is also the place in which mighty women have ruled their people since ancient times. In fact, some of these women were so good at calling the shots that the men who came after them decided to change their stories or wipe them out of history altogether!

Hatshepsut had the body of an ordinary woman, but she liked to show herself as big and muscular in images of her. This was the queen's way of telling the world that she was as powerful as any male ruler.

Hatshepsut, History's Hidden Pharaoh

Hatshepsut was one such awesome ruler. This impressive queen took control of Egypt at a time when rulers were almost always men. She made sure that no one would question her power by constantly showing her people that she was as great as any man.

Hatshepsut was born in 1479 BCE and was the daughter of the pharaoh Thutmose I. She married her half-brother, Thutmose II, when she was just 12 years old (pharaohs often had several wives, including close family) and had a daughter with him. When Hatshepsut's husband died, she quickly took control of Egypt and ruled it for her late husband's son, Thutmose III, who was still very young.

Taking Control

After seven years of Hatshepsut's rule, Thutmose III was almost old enough to become pharaoh. Knowing that she would lose her power if he took the throne, Hatshepsut announced that she was the pharaoh of Egypt and seized complete control.

Power Mad or Quick-thinking Queen?

In the past, many male historians have said that Hatshepsut seized power because she was ruthless and greedy. But in more recent years, historians have suggested that the queen could see that her stepson might be in danger if he became pharaoh because other relatives were eager to seize the throne. It may be that smart-thinking Hatshepsut knew that the only way to keep things stable was to stay in power herself.

When she became pharaoh, Hatshepsut ordered carvings and paintings of herself that showed her with a pharaoh's beard.

AS GOOD AS ANY MAN

Before Hatshepsut, only two other women had ruled Egypt in more than 1,500 years. Although Hatshepsut was not the very first female ruler, she was unusual in that she ruled the country with as much power as a man. Even her name tells us of her important role—it means, "She is first among noble women."

Smart and Ambitious

Hatshepsut was smart and made sure that she had good advisors to help her rule. She was also ambitious—she had many great buildings and structures created during her reign, including wonderful temples and magnificent **obelisks**.

Making Egypt Rich

Hatshepsut wanted to widen Egypt's power abroad too, so she sent Egyptians to faraway countries to **trade** with other **nations**. During her rule, important goods, such as spices and medicines, were brought back to Egypt from a distant land called Punt. It was probably the country that is now Eritrea, in Africa. The trade with other countries helped make Egypt even richer, which made Hatshepsut very popular.

No More Hatshepsut

Hatshepsut's rule lasted for 21 years, in which time she made Egypt peaceful, **prosperous**, and powerful. But on her death in 1458 BCE, her stepson Thutmose III took the throne and set about erasing any trace of Hatshepsut. He removed her name from monuments and got rid of many images of her.

One of Hatshepsut's greatest achievements was the huge temple she had built at Deir el-Bahri, on which her story and name is written.

You Can't Keep a Great Queen Down!

It was only when archaeologists began to figure out the **hieroglyphics** at Deir el-Bahri in the 1820s that Hatshepsut's story came to light. Then later, in 1903, Hatshepsut's tomb was also found, which revealed more information about this great ancient ruler. But there was still one great puzzle—Hatshepsut's mummified body was nowhere to be seen. It was not until 2007 that the mummy of Hatshepsut was finally found.

Today, the whole world knows the story of the mighty Egyptian pharaoh Hatshepsut and this once-hidden heroine is back in the headlines again.

HIDDEN HISTORY

Lost in the Past

Thutmose III probably **resented** the fact that his stepmother had ruled in his place. And he was likely uncomfortable with the idea that a woman had managed to rule as well as Hatshepsut. Whatever his reasons, Thutmose was determined to wipe the powerful queen from the pages of history, and for many centuries he succeeded.

Deir el-Bahri is one of the greatest buildings ever created in ancient Egypt.

Cleopatra, More than Just a Bob!

Today, if you ask people who Cleopatra was, they will likely tell you that she was a beautiful Egyptian queen with a glossy black bob. They might also tell you that she bathed in milk and that one of her boyfriends was the great Roman general Mark Antony. But there was far more to Cleopatra than that!

The Real Story

Like many other great female rulers, the true story of Cleopatra is rarely told. It began in Egypt around 70 BCE, when she was born. Cleopatra was the daughter of the Egyptian pharaoh Ptolemy XII. When she was just a teenager, Cleopatra married her much younger brother, Ptolemy XIII.

The couple was supposed to rule Egypt together. But Cleopatra had other ideas, so she made a daring move and declared herself the only ruler of Egypt. Cleopatra's bold act made her brother and husband furious, and in 49 BCE he drove her out of the capital of ancient Egypt, Alexandria.

Many images show Cleopatra with bobbed hair. In reality she had long hair and was ordinary looking, but not ordinary thinking.

Cleopatra fled from Egypt to the nearby country of Syria, where she set up her war camp.

Enter Julius Caesar

Meanwhile, back in Alexandria, the Roman emperor Julius Caesar was visiting Egypt. When Cleopatra heard that Caesar was in Egypt, she came up with a clever plan. She snuck back into the country and headed to Alexandria. When she got there, she told her servant to wrap her up in a carpet and then roll it out in front of Caesar.

I'm Impressed!

When Cleopatra appeared before Caesar, she begged him to help her. The emperor fell in love with Cleopatra and was so impressed by her that he decided to back her war. Cleopatra's brother fought back, but during the fighting, he drowned in the Nile River. Cleopatra then became queen.

> *Cleopatra knew that if she could win over the powerful Julius Caesar she might be able to win back her throne.*

HIDDEN HISTORY

Behind the Scenes

Cleopatra's act of rolling herself out of a carpet in front of Caesar has become famous in Hollywood movies, which show Cleopatra as a beautiful woman who loved to show off. The truth about Cleopatra is quite different. Her carpet act shows us that she was very smart and knew how to **manipulate** people.

Back to Business

As queen, Cleopatra was now free to get on with her ambition of making Egypt one of the greatest countries in the world. She traded with many different areas, including India and Arabia, to make sure that Egypt grew very rich. She also took back lands that Egypt had once owned, including large areas of Lebanon and Syria. Under Cleopatra's rule, Egypt grew into one of the greatest powers in the Mediterranean area.

A New Roman Boyfriend

When Caesar was killed, Cleopatra took another Roman boyfriend, the great Roman general Mark Antony. He was a very powerful man in the Roman Empire, which he helped control with a group of powerful men called the Senate. One of this group was Mark Antony's friend and Caesar's nephew, Octavian.

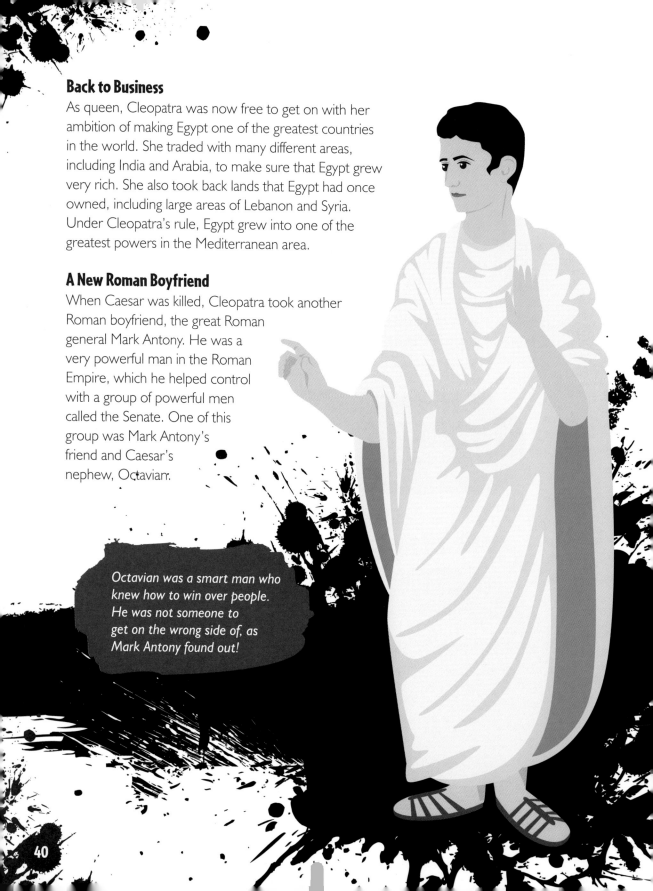

Octavian was a smart man who knew how to win over people. He was not someone to get on the wrong side of, as Mark Antony found out!

Hitting the Headlines

Unfortunately for Cleopatra, people in Rome were not happy that the Egyptian queen was carrying on with a married man—Mark Antony had a Roman wife, who was Octavian's sister! Mark Antony had also had three children with Cleopatra. Both Octavian and his sister were furious with Mark Antony and told him to stop the affair. When he refused, Octavian turned against him.

Mad, Bad, and Dangerous to Know!

Octavian used the bad press about Cleopatra as a gift to help topple her and Mark Antony. He told the Senate that Mark Antony was threatening the safety of the Roman Empire by having a relationship with a foreign ruler. The Romans then declared war on Egypt.

This Roman statue of Cleopatra shows her with a large nose. In reality Cleopatra was not a beauty, but it was her quick mind and engaging personality that made her Roman boyfriends, and her people, fall in love with her.

HIDDEN HISTORY

The True Face of a Queen

In the centuries that followed Cleopatra's rule, she became famous for being a gorgeous woman who rose to power because men fell in love with her beauty. However, when we look at artifacts that have images of the real Cleopatra on them, we see her power and attraction came from her intelligence and strategies.

This coin dating from 32 BCE shows Cleopatra. The queen liked to impress her people. She once even sailed up the Nile River dressed as an Egyptian goddess!

Fighting for Her Kingdom

With her rule under threat yet again, Cleopatra had no choice but to go to war against the Roman Empire. She even led her own fleet of ships into battle against the Romans in one fight.

Although she was a determined warrior queen, Cleopatra's army was no match for the mighty Roman army. As her fight to win the war began to fail, Cleopatra could see that it was all over for her. Rather than be captured by the Romans, in 30 BCE, she and Mark Antony took their own lives in Alexandria. The great reign of Cleopatra had come to an end.

Some stories say Cleopatra killed herself by being bitten by a snake called an asp, but no one knows for sure quite how she died.

We'll Change Her Story!

Even after her death, Cleopatra still got bad press from the Romans. Most Roman men were simply not comfortable with women being rulers—they just didn't believe that women were smart enough to grasp power. To keep Cleopatra from looking like the powerful ruler she was, Roman historians wrote that she had made Caesar and Mark Antony fall in love with her and then persuaded them to do whatever she wanted! In the centuries after Cleopatra's rule, this became the popular image of her in Europe.

HIDDEN HISTORY

The True Tale of a Smart Queen

The story told about Cleopatra in the Eastern world was quite different from that told in the West. Historical records from Central Asia say that she was amazingly smart and brilliant at math and science. She even met every week with a team of scientists to discuss her studies. Cleopatra could also speak at least nine languages, so she was able to talk to other rulers in different countries without needing an **interpreter**.

Roman women were not allowed to have power and Roman men made sure that they did exactly what they were told to do.

The Brainy Queen

Today, historians have uncovered the truth about Cleopatra and her real history is being told once more. We now know that she was a remarkable female ruler who turned Egypt into a superpower of its time. Her true tale really is a story of brains rather than beauty.

The Kandakes, the Coolest Queens Ever!

Most people know that Cleopatra was a famous African queen, and we now know that she took control in a man's world. But you probably don't know there was one kingdom in ancient Africa where it was perfectly normal for a woman to rule. In fact, in the kingdom of Kush, queens were right on trend!

From around 150 BCE, eight great queens ruled Kush. The great queens built their kingdom into a mighty power that traded with other peoples and built impressive buildings, including **pyramids**. They were also known as fearsome warrior queens who led their armies into battle.

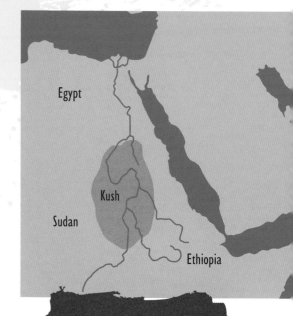

Egypt

Kush

Sudan

Ethiopia

Kush was an area in what is now Sudan. Under the rule of its powerful queens, the kingdom controlled a huge area of land, including modern-day Ethiopia, Sudan, and parts of Egypt.

The first queen was named Shanakdakhete, and she ruled from 170 to 150 BCE. Images of her often show her as a very large woman. Rather than being seen as a flaw, this was a sign of great power and wealth in Kush.

The queens of Kush were known as "kandake," which means queen and queen mother.

Amanishakheto ruled from 10 to 1 BCE. She was a powerful queen and is most famous for the pyramids and temples she built at Wad Naquaa, where she was buried with wonderful jewelry and many other treasures.

Other great kandakes include Amanitore, who ruled from 1 to 20 CE; Amantitere (22 to 41 CE); Amanikhatashan (62 to 85 CE); Maleqorobar (266 to 283 CE); and Lahideamani (306 to 314 CE), the last of the kandakes.

SHHH, DON'T TELL!

Many great stories about the kandakes and how they defeated their enemies have been told by the people of Kush and then passed down to their sons and daughters. One tells of how a kandake sent Alexander the Great packing when he tried to invade lands belonging to Kush. The story is that she led her army standing on the back of a giant elephant. She told Alexander that if he tried to invade, she would cut off his head and roll it down a hill! In the story, Alexander turned around and headed straight back home.

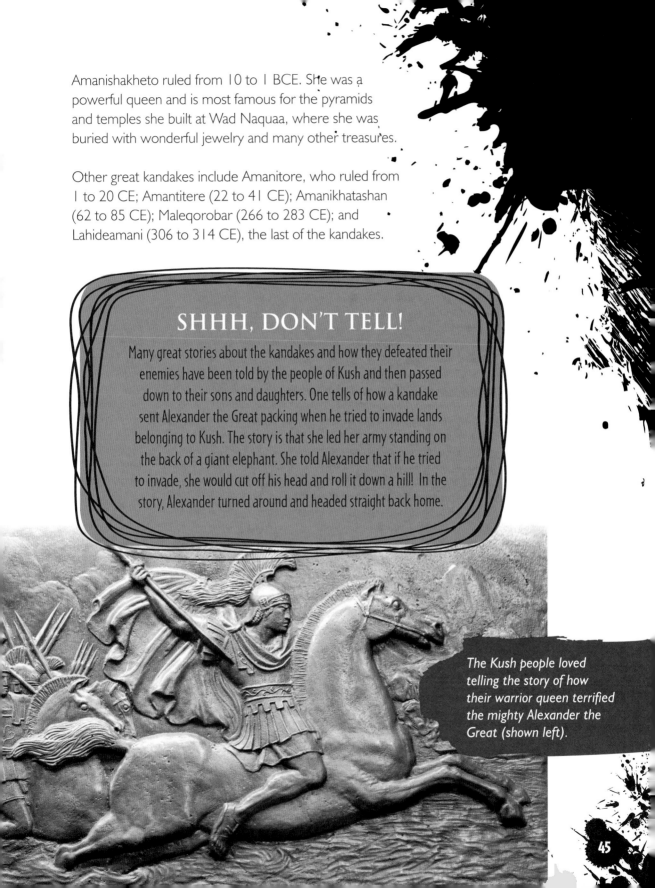

The Kush people loved telling the story of how their warrior queen terrified the mighty Alexander the Great (shown left).

GLOSSARY

abdicated Gave up the throne

alliance An agreement between two or more people or nations to help each other during war and conflicts

archaeologists People who examine buildings and objects left behind by people in the past to find out more about them

aristocracy Wealthy people at the top of society

authority Power over others

beheaded Had his or her head cut off

Catholic Related to the Catholic Church, which has the pope as its head

chancellor The chief minister of state in some European countries

Cherokee A Native American tribe

civilizations Organized groups of people

claim To say something belongs to oneself

conquerors People who take over other lands and their people by force

cultures Large groups of people who share the same language and ideas

death warrant A legal document ordering a person's death

epitaph Words that tell people about a person after his or her death

faith A belief in a spiritual power, for example, believing in Jesus and God

govern To organize people according to certain laws

heir A person who will become king or queen after the death of his or her parent king or queen

hieroglyphics A system of writing using pictures

illegitimate Born outside of marriage

interpreter A person who translates a language so that other people can understand what someone is saying

legal Related to the law

manipulate To make other people do as you wish

medieval A period of time between the fifth and fifteenth centuries

military commander A person in charge of armed forces

modernized Made modern

Mongol A person from Mongolia, an area to the west of China

Muslims People who believe in Allah and the prophet Muhammad

nations Large groups of people who live in one area and speak one language

noble Describes a person who was not from the poorer part of society and who often mixed with kings and queens

obelisks Ancient tall stone structures carved with pictures and words about important people who lived in the past

plot A secret plan

prenuptial Before a marriage

priests Men who are part of the Catholic Church and who lead religious ceremonies

productively Making a lot of something; making something quickly and well

prosperous Rich and wealthy

Protestants Christian people who believe in the Church of England

pyramids Large, four-sided structures shaped like an upside-down V and built in ancient times

recorded Written down

reign To rule, or the period of a person's rule

resented Felt angry about

rights Things a person should be allowed to do or allowed to have

settlers People who moved to a new country and began a new life there

societies Large groups of people who work and live together in an organized way

spy network A system of spies who all work together for one person or organization

steppes Large grassy areas in parts of Europe and Asia

taxes Money paid by people to a ruler or government

tortured Deliberately hurt

trade To exchange goods for other goods or for money

LEARNING MORE

Read more about women who broke the rules and changed the world!

Books

Bridges, Shirin Yim. *Hatshepsut of Egypt* (The Thinking Girl's Treasury of Real Princesses). Goosebottom Books, 2010.

Kramer, Barbara. *Cleopatra* (National Geographic Readers). National Geographic Kids, 2018.

Krull, Kathleen. *Lives of Extraordinary Women: Rulers, Rebels (and What the Neighbors Thought)*. Houghton Mifflin, 2013.

Rogers, Sam. *What's So Great About Queen Elizabeth I?: A Biography of Queen Elizabeth Just for Kids!* KidLit-O, 2014.

Websites

Learn more about the amazing queen Cleopatra at:
www.ducksters.com/history/ancient_egypt/cleopatra_vii.php

Discover more about the life of Hatshepsut at:
www.ducksters.com/history/ancient_egypt/hatshepsut.php

Read more about the life of Isabella of Castile at:
https://kids.kiddle.co/Isabella_of_Castile

Find out more about the amazing Wu Zetian at:
https://kids.kiddle.co/Wu_Zetian

Learn more about Elizabeth I at:
www.natgeokids.com/uk/discover/history/monarchy/elizabeth-i-facts

INDEX

ABOUT THE AUTHOR

Sarah Eason has written about science, geography, famous people, and history. She loves finding out about the past and the amazing people who lived long ago. In writing this book, she has discovered that there were many amazing women rulers in history, who all took on the world and showed them who was boss!